With love to our little angel, Zach
~ Mimi

# THE WISE ANIMAL HANDBOOK

## Kate B. Jerome

ARCADIA KIDS

Attempt new **skills** from **time** **to** **time.**

Just **try** to think them **through.**

# And if you find you're left behind....

...then change your point of view.

# Try not to think of just yourself.

**Invent** new ways to **Share.**

# Stay close to friends whom you can trust.

But always be **aware.**

# Avoid
### the
# tattle
### in the
# tale.

Insist that **truth** is **best**.

# Embrace with pride the strengths you have.

Demand
to be
impressed.

# Enjoy the peace that nature brings.

Ignore what's just for show.

# Join forces when the road gets rough.

**Admit** when you don't know.

# Remember
## family
### is the
## best.

Despite the ups and downs.

# Don't **hide** from things that you must **face.**

Make
joyful
laughing
sounds.

Eat
healthy
food to
grow
up
strong.

Be patient with your friends.

# Try not to take a stubborn stand.

Be **quick** to make **amends.**

# Excuse
yourself
when
manners
slip.

Be helpful every day.

# Keep trying even when it's hard.

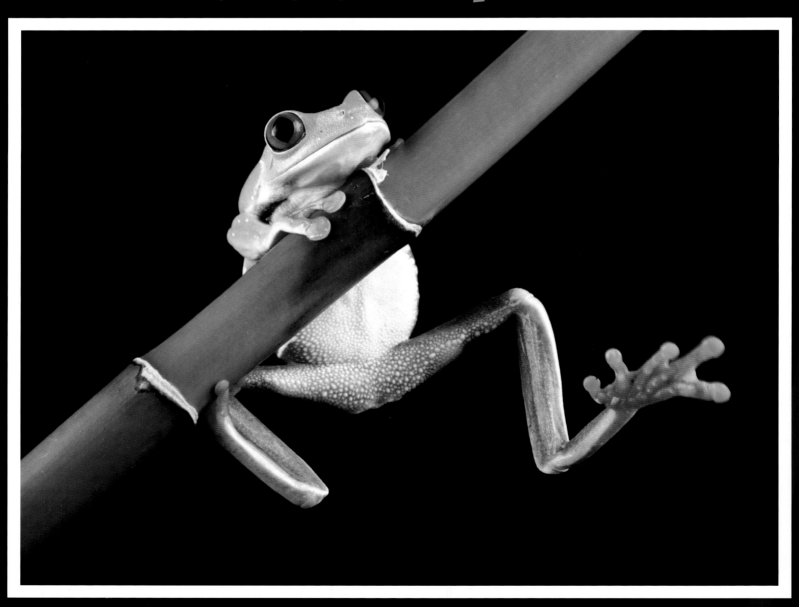

But don't forget to play!

# And
# sing

...and **dance** each **day!**

Written by Kate B. Jerome
Design and Production: Lumina Datamatics, Inc.
Coloring Illustrations: Tom Pounders
Research: Eric Nyquist

Cover Images: *See back cover*

Interior Images: 002 Anetapics/Shutterstock.com; 003 George Green/Shutterstock.com; 004 Sergey Uryadnikov/Shutterstock.com; 005 Gnomeandi/Shutterstock.com; 006 Bruce MacQueen/Shutterstock.com; 007 Henk Bentlage/Shutterstock.com; 008 M.M./Shutterstock.com; 009 Mikael Damkier/Shutterstock.com; 010 Brendan van Son/Shutterstock.com; 011 Michael Pettigrew/Shutterstock.com; 012 StevenRussellSmithPhotos/Shutterstock.com; 013 Pakhnyushchy/Shutterstock.com; 014 Patjo/Shutterstock.com; 015 Quinn Martin/Shutterstock.com; 016 Lincoln Rogers/Shutterstock.com; 017 Dirk Ercken/Shutterstock.com; 018 Karel Gallas/Shutterstock.com; 019 Orangecrush/Shutterstock.com; 020 Guenter-foto/Shutterstock.com; 021 Janecat/Shutterstock.com; 022 Shironina/Shutterstock.com; 023 Annette Shaff/Shutterstock.com; 024 Vitaly Titov/Shutterstock.com; 025 Rohappy/Shutterstock.com; 026 MattiaATH/Shutterstock.com; 027 Otsphoto/Shutterstock.com; 028 FikMik/Shutterstock.com; 029 Four Oaks/Shutterstock.com; 030 Ekaterina Kolomeets/Shutterstock.com; 031 Hugh Lansdown/Shutterstock.com.

Published by Arcadia Kids, a division of Arcadia Publishing and
The History Press, Charleston, SC

For all general information contact Arcadia Publishing at:
Telephone: 843-853-2070
Email: sales@arcadiapublishing.com

For Customer Service and Orders:
Toll Free: 1-888-313-2665
Visit us on the Internet at www.arcadiapublishing.com

Library of Congress Cataloging-in-Publication data is on file with the publisher.

Printed in China

# New Mexico State **Bird**

## Greater Roadrunner

**Read Together**

The roadrunner, also called the chaparral bird, prefers to walk or run than fly. It was named the state bird in 1949.

# New Mexico State Animal

## Black Bear

**Read Together** — The black bear was named the state animal in 1963. One of the most famous bears in the country, Smokey the Bear, was from New Mexico.

# New Mexico State **Insect**

## Tarantula Hawk Wasp

**Read Together**

The tarantula hawk wasp was named the state insect in 1989. Students at Edgewood Elementary School in Edgewood, NM, began the effort that led to the tarantula hawk wasp's top spot.

# New Mexico State Butterfly

## Sandia Hairstreak Butterfly

**Read Together**

The Sandia hairstreak butterfly was first discovered in La Cueva Canyon in Albuquerque in 1959. It became the state butterfly in 2003.